LIFTING

HEARTS

OFF

THE

GROUND

Lifting Hearts Off the Ground: Declaring Indigenous Rights in Poetry
Copyright © 2017 Lyla June Johnston & Joy De Vito

All Rights Reserved. No significant part of this publication may be reproduced, stored in a retrieval system, or transmitted in any form or in any means—by electronic, mechanical, photocopying, recording, or otherwise—without prior written permission. However, we welcome brief excerpts and quotations to be shared in books and articles, and on social media. We also welcome spoken sharing of these poems both in part and in whole.

The articles of the *United Nations Declaration on the Rights of Indigenous Peoples* are reprinted with the permission of the United Nations. A/RES/61/295 dated 13 September 2007 © United Nations.

Editor: Steve Heinrichs
Copy & Poetry Editor: Kyla Neufeld
Design & Layout: Jonathan Dyck
Publisher: Mennonite Church Canada

First Printing, 2017.
Printed by Friesens in Altona, Manitoba, Canada.
Treaty 1 Territory and the Homeland of the Métis Nation.

Library and Archives Canada Cataloguing in Publication

Lifting hearts off the ground : declaring indigenous rights in poetry / Lyla June Johnston & Joy De Vito.

Poems.
ISBN 978-0-9959733-0-5 (softcover)

1. Indigenous peoples--Civil rights--Poetry. I. Title: Declaring indigenous rights in poetry.

PS595.H76L54 2017   811'.6080355   C2017-903731-5

To the web of life.
To relatives with four legs, two legs, with wings,
who live in oceans, who live burrowed in the earth.
And within that web, to the human family,
that we might move towards reciprocal wholeness.
To those of us who suffer at the misguided hands of colonization,
may these words help and heal.
To those of us who inflict this suffering, both unwittingly and knowingly,
may these words enlighten, forgive, and educate.
To the Mothers, who were and are targeted
because they are the root of society.
To the Elders, who spoke outside of HIStory, before treaties
were forced upon us, on the terms of those who sought conquest.
To those who called out from the wilderness of
dehumanizing machines disguised as schools.
To the Warriors, who never gave up and will never give up.
To those who round dance in the streets!
To those Indigenous peoples of Europe who were similarly destroyed
and assimilated by patriarchy, fear, and other violent means.
To the healing of past and present wounds, that we might all
break free from the illusions of separation and hierarchy.
To the children born today, of every origin and background,
that they may know the Sacredness that created them,
and how Sacred they are.

Canada waged war against Indigenous peoples through law, and many of today's laws reflect that intent.... The full adoption and implementation of the *United Nations Declaration on the Rights of Indigenous Peoples* will not undo the War of Law, but it will begin to address that war's legacies.

— Senator Murray Sinclair, former Chief Commissioner of the Truth and Reconciliation Commission of Canada

For Healing and Life

Initiated by Indigenous peoples from around the world and negotiated with state representatives over the course of more than two decades, the *United Nations Declaration on the Rights of Indigenous Peoples* (2007) is a powerful proclamation of the principles that should guide Indigenous-Settler relations. Through its recognition of the inherent rights of Indigenous peoples — both their pre-existing collective human rights as peoples and nations, and the individual human rights of Indigenous children, women, men, and GLBTQ2 persons* — the *Declaration* offers a reparative antidote to the death-dealing colonial claims of past and present.

A handful of countries initially objected to the United Nations' adoption of the *Declaration* — including Canada and the United States. But by 2010 they had reversed their positions and the

---

*Although the *Declaration* does not explicitly name Indigenous gay, lesbian, bisexual, transgender, queer, and Two-Spirit (GLBTQ2) individuals, the rights of such persons are affirmed in, for example, Articles 2, 3, 9, and 12, which speak to the right to be free from discrimination, the right to self-determination, and the right to practice one's cultural traditions and customs.

Declaration achieved the status of a consensus instrument. Today, it's being used by domestic and international courts to interpret constitutions, legislation, and treaties; it's being lifted up by Indigenous peoples and Settler allies in relation to resource extraction, calling governments and corporations to honour the right of free, prior, and informed consent; and there are many grassroots communities, churches, and other faith bodies that are looking to the *Declaration* to help decolonize their relationships with host peoples in a good way.

It took a long time to get here. And we have a long way to go before we see real material shifts in the way Settler interactions with Indigenous peoples, cultures, and lands are lived out on the ground. But things are changing. More and more groups of people are coming together, seeking, finding, and practising ways of genuine respect.

Today, it is vital that all of us become conversant with the rights and minimum standards recognized in the *Declaration*. It's like the need to know the foundational stories of the lands we inhabit so that we can be fully present in our home place. It's like the need to know the intimacies of the watershed in which we live; to walk in loving solidarity with a world that's in ecological crisis, we've got to grow in that awareness. And so it is with the *Declaration* and relationships between Indigenous and Settler peoples. For far too long the hosts have been mistreated by the guests, living hearts pushed around and down by the structures of Settler society. We must radically re-examine the ways we relate in order to cast away injustice and do right by host peoples. The *Declaration* may not be the only tool to do such, but it's an indispensable one — essential for our collective well-being.

As Senator Murray Sinclair (Anishinaabe) puts it, the *Declaration* can help us address the legacies of legal warfare wrought by colonial powers. That war has caused so much damage, taking innumerable lives, wounding generations, and fracturing most homelands and territories. Ancient wisdom says, "As one part of the body suffers, we all suffer" (1 Corinthians 12:26). But heal that injured part, and the rest of the body receives gifts that mend and restore. Hence, the *Declaration* points to a way of living together that doesn't assert the fearful logic (present in so many of us Settlers) that we must bring one down in order to raise the other up. Not at all. We can rise together — Indigenous peoples, Settlers, and the land itself.

Yet note this. It's not only Indigenous peoples who are hurting and Indigenous lands that are in need of repair. "We've all been damaged by colonialism," says elder Stan McKay (Cree). "Our healing is different, but Settlers have to work through their stuff in order for us to mend the relationship." The *Declaration* is good news for everyone.

OH, HOW I LOVE YOUR LAW

The *Declaration* is not a long document — a short pre-amble and 46 articles. It doesn't take more than an hour to read. Yet I'm guessing most folks who do crack it open don't get past the first few pages. The language, though shaped by Indigenous narratives, perspectives, and principles, sounds like Western legalese and it's somewhat technical. That is important, for the *Declaration* is grounded in international law and needs to communicate to those who hold power. Yet for many, it's unfamiliar terrain that doesn't welcome us in. The words don't leap off the page; they don't grab one's heart and spirit. And that's what I long for — to find ways to hear and speak and imagine these words so that they come alive. How can we taste these rights; see their life; feel the weight of the past colonialism that birthed them; lament the present colonialism that makes them so urgent; celebrate the resilience of peoples who declare these legal standards to the watching world; and, in so doing, be transformed?

"Oh, how I love your law! I meditate on it all day long" (Psalm 119:97).

That's how an old poet in the Judeo-Christian tradition talked about Torah — the laws of Yahweh, the legal standards crafted by elders for the well-being of Israel's people. Some of the Hebrews thought these laws were so incredibly good that they were "more precious than gold; and sweeter than honey" (Psalm 19:10). Wouldn't it be awesome if we — both Indigenous and Settler — could say the same of the laws lifted up in the *Declaration*?

"Oh, how we love this *Declaration*; we rejoice in its statutes; how great a peace have we who follow its decrees!"

It's with that delicate and spirited hope that I invited two friends — Lyla June Johnston (Diné Bikéyah) and Joy De Vito (Settler Canadian) — to join hands and engage each article of the *Declaration* in a poetic conversation; to contemplate, wrestle with, and honour the text through story, question, intervention, and prayer so that the seemingly dry bones of the *Declaration* may be made alive in our eyes and in our relationships. So that hearts, once fallen to the ground, may be lifted high, together.

I am profoundly grateful to Lyla and Joy for their efforts. More will come to know and understand the *Declaration* because of their work. More will form relationships across Indigenous-Settler boundaries in response to their prayers. More will pursue that elusive form of reconciliation that we all need—one with justice, and even love.

> For the well-being of Indigenous peoples,
> and Settlers too,
> For the love of lands, waters, and
> all those ones-made-little.
> May the Spirit take these fragile words
> and breathe wheresoever she wills.

Steve Heinrichs
Director of Indigenous Relations
Mennonite Church Canada
Winnipeg
Treaty 1 Territory and the Homeland of the Métis Nation

NOTE TO THE READER

The articles of the *United Nations Declaration on the Rights of Indigenous Peoples* are typeset in Univers light.

Lyla June Johnston's poems are typeset in Scala regular.

Joy De Vito's poems are typeset in Scala italic.

I

Indigenous peoples have the right to the full enjoyment, as a collective or as individuals, of all human rights and fundamental freedoms as recognized in the Charter of the United Nations, the Universal Declaration of Human Rights, and international human rights law.

Am I uncivilized if I wear buckskin,
even while I pray for peace?
Are you civilized if you wear a wristwatch,
even as you wage war?

How do I quell the fears of my
sisters and brothers across the ocean?
How do I help them see that yes,
I am human?

How do we quell the anger in our hearts
when our humanness is questioned?
How do I replace this infinite frustration
with infinite forgiveness?

We will love in the face of the bloodshed,
in the face of hardships inflicted on a people
because we were purported to not
be People.

We will hold fast to love,
to forgiveness,
to truth.

We anxiously await the day
when they don't need declarations
and articles to know that yes,

indeed,
we are human.

I see beauty in movement.
Trees pulsating to
the whisper of breeze
that trails the swaying grass.
I see beauty in the movement of creation.

Yet,
to my dismay,
I can remain unmoved by humanity.
I rarely celebrate the rights
that are the foundation of
my comfort.

Why do I struggle to grasp beauty
everywhere,
in everyone?

2

ARTICLE 2

Indigenous peoples and individuals are free and equal to all other peoples and individuals and have the right to be free from any kind of discrimination, in the exercise of their rights, in particular that based on their indigenous origin or identity.

The old ones say:

Creator writes your rights
in the pages of
your life.

Read them in
the stars.

Listen to the voice
of the earth
when the snow melts
and the soil exhales.

She will help you understand:

You have no "rights" but
the right
to choose love

or choose fear.

I immediately protest:
   Of course you're equal,
   don't accuse me of that.
Yet it needs to be written down.
   It's the way I see myself as the norm.
   It needs to be written down.

3

Indigenous peoples have the right to self-determination. By virtue of that right they freely determine their political status and freely pursue their economic, social, and cultural development.

If you tell a deer enough times
that she is a bear,
she will believe it.

If you tell a woman enough times
that she is a slave,
she will believe it.

No more.
Don't coddle me
with commodity foods,
free "healthcare,"
free "education."

They are shackles.

Now, even the Indian Stanford grad
isn't smart enough to see:
civilization does not lie
in the conqueror's mansion
built by bones of those not yet born,

but in the wonder of
ways so old
they're new.

The trick is to determine your destiny

based on the understanding
that you are women,

not slaves.

Choices are freedom.
We take ours for granted
and choice turns to burden, a stress.
If you are not allowed to determine your future,
does desperation turn to resignation?
How easily we forget.

4

Indigenous peoples, in exercising their right to self-determination, have the right to autonomy or self-government in matters relating to their internal and local affairs, as well as ways and means for financing their autonomous functions.

There are frescos of blue coats
pointing rifles into the backs of
Diné women
on the walls of the
"Navajo Nation"
council chambers.

We became caricatures
of the oppressor.
We look so sad and ridiculous,
trying to write laws on pieces of paper
when we know the law of stars,
the law of rain,
the law of women as life-bearers.

I don't care if his skin is brown
and his last name is Tsosie.
If our president is sold to extraction
we are not self-governed,
but governed by the rhythms of greed.

Let the women lead as they did for
generations.
Let us taste true self-governance.

We could let go of purse strings,
and bankrupt the market that demands
financial gain regardless of the cost
to creation.

We could untangle the knots of legislation
that evaluate everything, from education to land,
and confound attempts
at relationship.

We could question the Western
philosophy that views
the advancement of "civilization"
as progress.

But we would have to give up our cherished images of
   parent,
   patron,
   power.

5
&
6

ARTICLE 5

Indigenous peoples have the right to maintain and strengthen their distinct political, legal, economic, social, and cultural institutions, while retaining their right to participate fully, if they so choose, in the political, economic, social, and cultural life of the State.

ARTICLE 6

Every indigenous individual has the right to a nationality.

An Anishinaabeg woman
ventures to a grand place they
call Harvard.

She has this piece of paper
that says she is a citizen
of this grand thing they
call America.

She has earned the respect of her colonizer.
She comes home in the winters
for something they
call Christmas.

The words of her grandmother,
spoken in a mother tongue,
are harder
and harder
to understand.

Distinct institutions and state participation:
a primal fear
masked by the language of
  finances,
  land,
  nationality.

Though I refuse any designation other than "Canadian,"
I rarely consider the offering of belonging.
My family has been here so long
that our original land was a grant.
A nationality established on the identity of another.
Why are we so threatened by the
traditions of another people?

7

1. Indigenous individuals have the rights to life, physical and mental integrity, liberty, and security of person.

2. Indigenous peoples have the collective right to live in freedom, peace, and security as distinct peoples and shall not be subjected to any act of genocide or any other act of violence, including forcibly removing children of the group to another group.

It's 1940. The truant officer's boots glisten with
morning dew.

"Run," mother says.

Thanks to the back door,
I never went to White Man's
school.

It's 2017. The truant officer wears a college recruiter
disguise.

He seduces me with stories of
civilization and savagery.

If only our children saw the permittivity of:
monocrops
aquifer depletion
nuclear waste
reef destruction
selling the meat of our own umbilical chord,

they would be home by now,
firelight streaking across their faces,
winter stories travelling deep into their hearts.

If a stranger knocked on my door for my kids,
how would I breathe
if I had been taken from my own parents?
Each generation knowing,
and not knowing,
where the next one was being taken.
And we offer protection from genocide?

8

1. Indigenous peoples and individuals have the right not to be subjected to forced assimilation or destruction of their culture.

2. States shall provide effective mechanisms for prevention of, and redress for:

   a. Any action which has the aim or effect of depriving them of their integrity as distinct peoples, or of their cultural values or ethnic identities;

   b. Any action which has the aim or effect of dispossessing them of their lands, territories, or resources;

   c. Any form of forced population transfer which has the aim or effect of violating or undermining any of their rights;

   d. Any form of forced assimilation or integration;

   e. Any form of propaganda designed to promote or incite racial or ethnic discrimination directed against them.

It's 1958 and a Hopi toddler is being
shipped like freight to
Riverside, California.

Today the superintendent slapped
his hand red
for speaking
the mother tongue.

The sun is setting.
Hopi boy and palm tree silhouettes.
An odd combination.

He is crying.
He is crying.

An older boy sits down to comfort him.
"Um waynuma?" he whispers.

He responds:
"Owí, nu' waynuma."

Every few years we wring our hands
because we can't define "Canadian."
We can only muster that we
> *are not brash,*
> *aggressive,*
> *loud.*

We carry the mantle of gentility as we
> *quietly assume the authority*
in unbalanced relationships.

Yet there are some
meeting in small groups.
Settlers who question the norm.
Seeking to disrupt
the seductive vision
of uniformity.

9

Indigenous peoples and individuals have the right to belong to an indigenous community or nation, in accordance with the traditions and customs of the community or nation concerned. No discrimination of any kind may arise from the exercise of such a right.

It's the year 2598:
The last remaining descendent of the Narragansett
has white skin and blue eyes.

Her great, great grandmother told her grandmother
tales of The People.

Does she belong? She doesn't "look Indian" to them.
But who will carry the stories if not her?

It's 3 a.m. and she wants to write a book.
Stories about The People.
Society mutters in her mind and
she cannot lift the pen.

It's 2017 and the casino is doing well,
fleecing the poor.
Driving my grandmother mad.

The council has decided that all members
with less than "one fourth"
blood quantum are taken off rosters.

The Tribal Chairman can buy that new car now.
One day, people with pale skin will be more "Indian" than him.

July 1.
Traditions and customs.
The roots of Indigenous community
   reduced to colourful displays
   for "Canada Day."
An unsettling alignment of
   an attempt to claim a shared heritage,
   an unabashed celebration of superiority.
We seek the protection of our rights,
   celebrate another's culture when it suits,
and dismiss those who refuse to conform.

IO

ARTICLE 10

Indigenous peoples shall not be forcibly removed from their lands or territories. No relocation shall take place without the free, prior, and informed consent of the indigenous peoples concerned and after agreement on just and fair compensation and, where possible, with the option of return.

If you separate
The People
from the land,

their bodies may live,
but The People
will die.

She weaves our languages together
with grassy plain glottal stops and
buffalo breath.

You can separate us
from the land but
then we will have
nothing to speak about.

We will remain in this land
or The People will perish.

Indian Affairs, 1969, White Paper logics:
    forced relocation for the good of the community.
A former Prime Minister, 2016:
    "sometimes people have to move."

Sitting behind a desk,
removed from the reserve,
is the best place to make such a decision
(it helps if you don't witness the turmoil).
Benevolence is a front for sovereignty.
    The disorientation is intentional.

II

1. Indigenous peoples have the right to practice and revitalize their cultural traditions and customs. This includes the right to maintain, protect, and develop the past, present and future manifestations of their cultures, such as archaeological and historical sites, artefacts, designs, ceremonies, technologies, and visual and performing arts and literature.

2. States shall provide redress through effective mechanisms, which may include restitution, developed in conjunction with indigenous peoples, with respect to their cultural, intellectual, religious, and spiritual property taken without their free, prior, and informed consent or in violation of their laws, traditions, and customs.

Potlatch season is here. The dances are clearing
the streets of fear. The smell of smoked
salmon fills the air.
But why does our generosity scare
the palefaces so? How could an open hand
be confused with a threat or weapon?

Our hands our open.
Our hands are open.
Our hands are open
to the sky, receiving the gifts of rain
and returning them to the earth,
to the people.

The man that gives away all his possessions
is the highest king. The man that loves
and respects women,
the most decorated warrior.

We are told the man
who accumulates the most,
and controls the bodies
of the most women
is the highest king.

But these kings follow the flow
of the queens. The mothers

are the creators and we are singing
about their force and power.
We are singing about their love
and generosity.

Why have these songs been silenced?
Because they render
the whole operation of colonialism
unnecessary and jejune
in the face of just
one step of her dance, one beat
of her drum, one smile
on my child's face.

The manifestations of many cultures
sit behind glass in museums.
Intricate beadwork woven with care
now labelled an artefact,
identified only by the
name of the Settler collector.
Fragments of ceremonies
separated from purpose
to act as teaching tools of the colonizer.
Viewers rush to the next exhibit,
learning their history.

12

1. Indigenous peoples have the right to manifest, practice, develop, and teach their spiritual and religious traditions, customs, and ceremonies; the right to maintain, protect, and have access in privacy to their religious and cultural sites; the right to the use and control of their ceremonial objects; and the right to the repatriation of their human remains.

2. States shall seek to enable the access and/or repatriation of ceremonial objects and human remains in their possession through fair, transparent, and effective mechanisms developed in conjunction with indigenous peoples concerned.

We speak wonderful
words of rights and freedoms
as the bones of ancestors meet the teeth
of the dozer.

It's time to put in a pipeline.
We, the developers of "progress,"
are trying not to care.
We are trying to make it look like we do.

The black snake must go through.
The investors told us so.

The attempted erasure of a people
depended on the banning of ceremony.
    The memories and traditions were
    too powerful to ignore.

Dismiss the potlatch as a simple dance
and imprison the bodies of those who participate.
Force spirituality underground
    into hiding
        where only a few are aware of its truth.
Silence
where once there were celebrations of life.

13

ARTICLE 13

1. Indigenous peoples have the right to revitalize, use, develop, and transmit to future generations their histories, languages, oral traditions, philosophies, writing systems, and literatures, and to designate and retain their own names for communities, places, and persons.

2. States shall take effective measures to ensure that this right is protected and also to ensure that indigenous peoples can understand and be understood in political, legal, and administrative proceedings, where necessary through the provision of interpretation or by other appropriate means.

The Maori warrior is speaking
his language to the eel.
They understand him.
He understands them.

Come out
of your dwelling,
furnished with Chinese pleather
and important-looking pictures.
Step onto the land.
Understand. The eel and I
have a story for you
about beauty and providence.

The stories must be maintained.
How might we make space for you
to breathe life into the words
*   snatched by education?*
To hear names
*   no longer kept hidden?*

14

ARTICLE 14

1. Indigenous peoples have the right to establish and control their educational systems and institutions providing education in their own languages, in a manner appropriate to their cultural methods of teaching and learning.

2. Indigenous individuals, particularly children, have the right to all levels and forms of education of the State without discrimination.

3. States shall, in conjunction with indigenous peoples, take effective measures, in order for indigenous individuals, particularly children, including those living outside their communities, to have access, when possible, to an education in their own culture and provided in their own language.

She has her moccasin on one foot
and a high heel on the other.
They tied her hair
in ceremonial fashion
when her first blood came.
Taught her what it means to be
a relative of the rain. She is

solving derivatives by day
and healing the sick
with ancient songs by night.

She is writing her treatise
on the beauty of ceremonial
discovery. Some call it research.

She is defending her dissertation.
She is defending her land.
Defending her water.
She has come
to learn. But more so,
she has come to teach the world
the beauty in her people's language.

*Witness the beauty of language
as it widens the circle of understanding
to include knowledge of
   self and community,
   land and life.*

15

1. Indigenous peoples have the right to the dignity and diversity of their cultures, traditions, histories, and aspirations which shall be appropriately reflected in education and public information.

2. States shall take effective measures, in consultation and cooperation with the indigenous peoples concerned, to combat prejudice and eliminate discrimination and to promote tolerance, understanding, and good relations among Indigenous peoples and all other segments of society.

The sweat lodge door closes
and the drum
kicks up. The spirits are flooding
in as the water splashes
the red hot rocks.

My grandmother tells me
when the door closes and the womb
is dark, there is no race. We are all
children of the mystery.
Red People. Black People.
White People. Yellow People.
All have come to dance
in the sacred arbour.

When each hoop is represented,
my grandmother says
it is an auspicious time.
My grandmother says
we all have the same
colour of palm. The colour of flesh
and blood and bone.
Together we are made whole.
We look to the skies and see
the many different kinds of birds
roosting in the trees. I am so glad
Creator gave us so many feathers
to admire.

What would the Eagle be
without all the other bird sisters
to take care of?
What would the world be
with only pigeons? Each colour
of skin is sacred and beautiful.

Europeans: you are held to this.
Each colour of skin is sacred and beautiful.

Turtle Islanders: you are held to this.
I have been slighted by my brethren
and sistren for taking a paleface
into my home and feeding them.

Turtle Islanders: your painful past
does not permit you to throw
the same poison
back across the ocean.
Each is held to this truth.

> *Do I dare acknowledge a role in the state?*
> *Do I need to respond?*
> *Tolerance and dignity will not be*
> *legislated into existence.*
> *Respect is lived into being.*

16

1. Indigenous peoples have the right to establish their own media in their own languages and to have access to all forms of non-indigenous media without discrimination.

2. States shall take effective measures to ensure that State-owned media duly reflect indigenous cultural diversity. States, without prejudice to ensuring full freedom of expression, should encourage privately owned media to adequately reflect indigenous cultural diversity.

I am a child of the earth. #Keyah.
I am a warrior for the earth. #NihimaNahasdzáán.
I am interdependent with the earth. #ToNihimá.
I belong to the earth. #ÁhaNasha.

We would have typed it faster if our iPhones
spoke Diné Bizaad, the Navajo language.
There will be a day when we will not
be auto-corrected out of existence.

Heartbreaking and infuriating by turns.
Turn on the latest blockbuster, switch to the news,
and watch the caricatures played out
  for laughs,
  for pity.
Art is necessary:
  the crier of reality,
  the pursuer of dreams,
  the voice of expression.
Yet, far too often,
  the voice of the majority.

17

1. Indigenous individuals and peoples have the right to enjoy fully all rights established under applicable international and domestic labour law.

2. States shall in consultation and cooperation with indigenous peoples take specific measures to protect indigenous children from economic exploitation and from performing any work that is likely to be hazardous or to interfere with the child's education, or to be harmful to the child's health or physical, mental, spiritual, moral, or social development, taking into account their special vulnerability and the importance of education for their empowerment.

3. Indigenous individuals have the right not to be subjected to any discriminatory conditions of labour and, *inter alia*, employment or salary.

Come closer to me. I want to drink tea
with you. I want to eat
with you. I want to laugh
with you. I've been working
in the diamond fields
all day and you're 8,000 miles away.

You've formalized your family
with a sparkling ring.
Your husband and your children
are eating a meal.
Can you see me?
You are with your family now,
eating dinner. But still, you are not
with all your family.
My skin is ebony but I am still your child,
mother. The London PR office shields me
from your view.

Come closer, mother.
I want to drink tea with you.
I want to eat with you.
I want to laugh with you.

The market protects me from learning how much
my comfort rests on the backs of others.
My cheap clothes come at great cost to an ignored worker.
I buy used, convincing myself that one person
circumventing the system makes a difference.

Careful thought shows, this is not enough.
But I can't get up now.
I'm busy assembling my new chair
that came in the mail.

18

Indigenous peoples have the right to participate in decision-making in matters which would affect their rights, through representatives chosen by themselves in accordance with their own procedures, as well as to maintain and develop their own indigenous decision making institutions.

Ben Nighthorse-Campbell is
a Republican from Colorado.
A Native American politician.
I saw him on a poster
in the Bureau of Indian Education
school I went to as a child once.
He is trying his best
in an institution
built on his mother's bones.
How do we break free?
Our institution built on ceremony
has been eclipsed from the earth.
Or has it?

You can hear the night chanters
way out in the desert. They are singing
about democracy
in our own language.
We need you to come into our Inipi.
The legislator is in session.
The speaker of the house is on her knees
praying for the children.
The lobbyists are wafting cedar
smoke onto their faces.
The judge proclaims us all innocent
as she transforms from liquid into steam.
The laws are written in a bent-willow alphabet.

Come. Come and learn
how to read them.

We learn of decisions denied
when the rules of the colonizer are enforced.
The National Parks Commission tells us
   "appreciate nature here"
and we tent on burial grounds.
The promise of high returns
drives development
deeper and deeper into the land.
Laws must be passed to ensure
that no child is left untreated.

Our institutions
rarely spark the imagination
that is required to
see a different path.

19

ARTICLE 19

States shall consult and cooperate in good faith with the indigenous peoples concerned through their own representative institutions in order to obtain their free, prior, and informed consent before adopting and implementing legislative or administrative measures that may affect them.

The oldest woman. The mother of all.
She birthed the next generation,
with sweat building on her brow, hanging on
to the belt hanging from the roof. The belt
her mother gave her at 13 winters.

Squatting, never laying on her back, she birthed
the next generation in the context of ceremony
and song. If you wish to consult
with our representative institution,
then go to her. She will help you
understand what the next generation
will need.

Confess it:
free, prior, and informed consent
disarms powers and shatters structures.
It acknowledges hosts
    and the etiquette of guests.
It assumes equality in discussion.
    The right to information.
    The right to say "no."
The colonizer's "yes" has always been the answer
    to the questions never asked.

20

1. Indigenous peoples have the right to maintain and develop their political, economic, and social systems or institutions, to be secure in the enjoyment of their own means of subsistence and development, and to engage freely in all their traditional and other economic activities.

2. Indigenous peoples deprived of their means of subsistence and development are entitled to just and fair redress.

It's the first whale hunt
in 60 years. The people. Do they remember
how to do it?
The environmentalists are telling them to stop
(while they explore fine-dining
and drive their motorcars).

The harpoon is shooting out
like a lightning bolt. Guided
by something we were told about
but have never known. Until now.

The whale gives itself to you. It could get away
if it wanted. We are cutting its body
into hundreds of pieces
and practising nulch'ahn'tah.
Some people call it economics.
Some people call it fulfillment
of the human spirit. To give, to love, to be.

I see the children smiling
for the first time in weeks.
I see the grandfather full
of a joy he cannot express. Glad
we gave him one more chance to hunt
before he closes those eyes forever.
Some people call it subsistence.

Some call it a great circle.
We are stuck in this infinity, joyfully stuck
in the cycle Creator made
for the water, the soil, the bodies, the plants,
and the stones.

Eleven lives.

They jolted the consciousness of some
into recognizing the roots
of despair.

Eleven lives.

Exposed the gaping wound
left when a collective past
is erased.

Eleven suicides attempted
in 24 hours
in Attawapiskat.

We talk about subsistence and forget
that for some
the fight is for
survival.

21

ARTICLE 21

1. Indigenous peoples have the right, without discrimination, to the improvement of their economic and social conditions, including, *inter alia*, in the areas of education, employment, vocational training and retraining, housing, sanitation, health, and social security.

2. States shall take effective measures and, where appropriate, special measures to ensure continuing improvement of their economic and social conditions. Particular attention shall be paid to the rights and special needs of indigenous elders, women, youth, children, and persons with disabilities.

Nine generations ago the smell
of gunpowder lingered in the nightmares
of Hochungra mothers. Don't worry,
blood spilled into rivers will disappear
over time.

The people born of crisis are living
in a place they call La Crosse, Wisconsin.
People wonder why they are so poor.
Why they eat so unhealthy.
Why they drink so much alcohol.

They wonder these things
over the brim of wine glasses
from a balcony overlooking the valleys
where The People's blood
has since vanished.

They wonder these things
and they will sleep warm tonight.
They will be fed tonight.

The nightly news walks past the desperation.
A quick glance at the ongoing trauma.
Guilt says, "Do something!"
But dirty water is forgotten
when it runs clean at home.

ARTICLE 22

1. Particular attention shall be paid to the rights and special needs of indigenous elders, women, youth, children, and persons with disabilities in the implementation of this Declaration.

2. States shall take measures, in conjunction with indigenous peoples, to ensure that indigenous women and children enjoy the full protection and guarantees against all forms of violence and discrimination.

I met a girl in Florida once.
She was a Lakota.

"You're a long way from home," I said.

"I know," she said.

"How did you get here?" I asked.

"The government took me
from my mom and put me in a foster home
in St. Petersburg."

It's the second millennium
and our children are still being stolen?

She tells me her foster brothers used to touch
her in uncomfortable places.
Tonight she is going to the strip club to work.

Lakotas and palm trees don't mix.
But here they try to survive together
in a foreign land.
I wish it was a hypothetical story.
But I met her on a day
they call January 13, 2017.

Be silent.
Hear the agonizing cries
of the overpowered.
Mourn.
Cut out the tumour
from the system whose anatomy
is violence.

23

ARTICLE 23

Indigenous peoples have the right to determine and develop priorities and strategies for exercising their right to development. In particular, indigenous peoples have the right to be actively involved in developing and determining health, housing, and other economic and social programmes affecting them and, as far as possible, to administer such programmes through their own institutions.

"When are you going to let others
decide the fate of your children.
Are you not warriors?"

This message came like thunder
to Mr. Tilsen, a man of the plains.

The children are out harvesting
Timsila root. The houses are
medicine wheels fusing the best of all colours
to create a sustainable storm.
Those voluptuous clouds
full of static and water hover
over the waiting mouths.
Those bolts of lightning flashing across the sky
remind The People of their sophistication.

The White Man said we would need him.
We knew the day would come
when he saw that he needed us.

Agency,
  the right to choose.
Activity,
  the freedom to move.
Actualized,
  by those with lived experience.
Reverse,
  solutions ordained by the outside.
Experience alternatives.

24

ARTICLE 24

1. Indigenous peoples have the right to their traditional medicines and to maintain their health practices, including the conservation of their vital medicinal plants, animals, and minerals. Indigenous individuals also have the right to access, without any discrimination, to all social and health services.

2. Indigenous individuals have an equal right to the enjoyment of the highest attainable standard of physical and mental health. States shall take the necessary steps with a view to achieving progressively the full realization of this right.

Sweet cedar smoke curls
into the midnight sky.

The songs of the people are entering
our bodies, teaching each cell,
each strand of DNA,
about beauty and wonder.

It is this phosphoric chant,
visible only to closed eyes,
that weaves in between our dreams,
sewing our consciousness to the sky.
Through this beauty we find
a world inside the world.

We arise at dawn
once the ceremony is complete,
like newborns are born of a womb.

Viewing tradition as a mysticism that threatens the system
means that well-being comes at a cost.
*   Story, ceremony, and healing are silenced*
*   in hospitals that recognize only Western science.*
Paperwork and forms transmit information with
proof of illness in point form.
*   Spirituality and personhood*
*   dissolved by the system.*

Indigenous peoples have the right to maintain and strengthen their distinctive spiritual relationship with their traditionally owned or otherwise occupied and used lands, territories, waters, and coastal seas and other resources and to uphold their responsibilities to future generations in this regard.

It's October 27, 2016
in Cannonball, North Dakota.
Rubber bullets thud. My brother
coughs up blood.
Bravery and grace stand to the mace,
sprayed in the face with the foul taste of hate.

Seems like we've been here before.
A chemical war.
Choppers and planes fly low, so low
they can hear our prayers for them.
For our water.
For our children.
For a world lost in fear.

Through it all we know
nature will have the last word.
We will perish apart
from the sweet river bank of truth:
the truth of the perfection of Creator's design.

Let us back into the lands of our grandmothers
and we will show you the way home.

The land is the great divide. "We" structured
ourselves around the promise
of the land as security,
never questioning if it was intended to be
our keeper.

1. Indigenous peoples have the right to the lands, territories, and resources which they have traditionally owned, occupied, or otherwise used or acquired.

2. Indigenous peoples have the right to own, use, develop, and control the lands, territories, and resources that they possess by reason of traditional ownership or other traditional occupation or use, as well as those which they have otherwise acquired.

3. States shall give legal recognition and protection to these lands, territories, and resources. Such recognition shall be conducted with due respect to the customs, traditions, and land tenure systems of the indigenous peoples concerned.

The wind slides between branches,
playing the leaves like a gayageum.
A parting song.

The Korean forest stands still as night.
Awaiting its death.
Japan's blind teeth are gnashing,
too far away to hear her song.
The king's moustache is stained
with rice and broth as he speaks in lies:
"Liberation and progress."

You are not here to help us.
You are here to rip the hair
of the earth from its scalp and burn it all
to fuel your escaping, short-sighted dream.
We sing prayers to the soil
that holds the forest, knowing
that from these ashes
she will be born again.

Blustering, terrified, angry, protective.
We extract resources and promises with reckless abandon;
believing oil, trees, potash, and salmon
affirm our sovereignty, our only hope.
But, if we stop,
the silence might speak.
If we listen,
we may learn:
"Do not fear."

27

ARTICLE 27

States shall establish and implement, in conjunction with indigenous peoples concerned, a fair, independent, impartial, open, and transparent process, giving due recognition to indigenous peoples' laws, traditions, customs, and land tenure systems, to recognize and adjudicate the rights of indigenous peoples pertaining to their lands, territories, and resources, including those which were traditionally owned or otherwise occupied or used. Indigenous peoples shall have the right to participate in this process.

There are laws and there are laws.
Some of us have forgotten
that ink on paper can be burned, torn,
obeyed, and disobeyed.
Other laws, written into bone
and sand, are more lovable and lasting.

Love says she is the judge of judges.
Without her we will perish.
Not as punishment,
but as natural fact.

Traditions forced into one legal system
lose their life.
We examine the individual
    and miss the offering of community.
Legal jargon obscures emotions
    and softens the necessary acknowledgment of pain.
Punishment is sought as the solution
    and the life-giving traditions of reconciliation
    are excluded.

28

1. Indigenous peoples have the right to redress, by means that can include restitution or, when this is not possible, just, fair, and equitable compensation, for the lands, territories, and resources which they have traditionally owned or otherwise occupied or used, and which have been confiscated, taken, occupied, used, or damaged without their free, prior, and informed consent.

2. Unless otherwise freely agreed upon by the peoples concerned, compensation shall take the form of lands, territories and resources equal in quality, size, and legal status or of monetary compensation or other appropriate redress.

And so, when you are ready
to step into the court of stars,
with God as your advocate,
we will be waiting.
Near the dead stumps of the old
Korean forest we will be waiting for you.

Together we will plant seeds that nourish
the future. The love we share
will nourish us both,
liberating colonized and colonizer
from the chains of fear and hatred.

Redress, restitution, compensation:
terrifying promises for those who place trust in
    our livelihood,
    our houses,
    our economy,
    our land.
We are afraid there is not enough,
    that we will reap what we have sown.

29

ARTICLE 29

1. Indigenous peoples have the right to the conservation and protection of the environment and the productive capacity of their lands or territories and resources. States shall establish and implement assistance programmes for indigenous peoples for such conservation and protection, without discrimination.

2. States shall take effective measures to ensure that no storage or disposal of hazardous materials shall take place in the lands or territories of indigenous peoples without their free, prior, and informed consent.

3. States shall also take effective measures to ensure, as needed, that programmes for monitoring, maintaining, and restoring the health of indigenous peoples, as developed and implemented by the peoples affected by such materials, are duly implemented.

The land is a mirror,
sometimes reflecting beauty,
sometimes reflecting death.
In cleansing the land we are cleansed.
In healing the land we are healed.

I sat all day looking at the eyes
inscribed on aspen tree skin.
She looked at me, I looked at her.
All day long she showed me my own beauty.
We become who we are surrounded by.
The land made him a better man.

"Not in my backyard."
The prerogative of suburbanites
in response to everything from wind farms to dumps.
Hazardous materials?
Never considered.

What of those who have no say?
The government studies whether the poisons
already dumped
need to be cleaned.
Mercury, it is written, might not be harmful.

1. Military activities shall not take place in the lands or territories of indigenous peoples, unless justified by a relevant public interest or otherwise freely agreed with or requested by the indigenous peoples concerned.

2. States shall undertake effective consultations with the indigenous peoples concerned, through appropriate procedures and in particular through their representative institutions, prior to using their lands or territories for military activities.

Without firing a single bullet
they have defeated the largest military
might on earth. They fought
with truth. They fought with prayer.
They fought with joy.
Vieques is singing victory songs.

They have defeated
their own hatred for "the colonizer."
They have forgiven their foe.
They are dancing all around the pain
proclaiming it impotent and dead.

Freedom on the bioluminescent shores
they dance.
They are dancing with
feet of strength.
Feet of love.
A feat of wonder.

Colonialism does not require muscular violence
to be maintained.
The weapons of land claims, capitalism,
and superiority
cloaked as recognition
negotiate
to protect the system.

ARTICLE 31

1. Indigenous peoples have the right to maintain, control, protect, and develop their cultural heritage, traditional knowledge and traditional cultural expressions, as well as the manifestations of their sciences, technologies, and cultures, including human and genetic resources, seeds, medicines, knowledge of the properties of fauna and flora, oral traditions, literatures, designs, sports and traditional games, and visual and performing arts. They also have the right to maintain, control, protect, and develop their intellectual property over such cultural heritage, traditional knowledge, and traditional cultural expressions.

2. In conjunction with indigenous peoples, States shall take effective measures to recognize and protect the exercise of these rights.

The old ones say we do not own
the land, much less the songs,
much less the symbols gifted to us
by the star nation.

Who can own the only thing worth having?
Who can own God?

The Lakota were the most generous
of us. Freely giving their sacred technology
to all who asked for it. To all who needed it.

Take it. Take it for we cannot hoard
what was freely given to us.
Try to sell it. Try to exploit it.
Try to patent it. Try to own it.
Try it.

The moment you think you own it
is the moment it disappears, slipping
through your fingers like holy water.
You cannot hold it.
Only you can be held by it.
We do not carry this sacred pipe.
It carries us. Through the valleys,
and over the hills.
It cannot be owned. You can only pretend

to own it, just like you pretend
to own your own flesh and bone.
Can't take it with us on the soul's journey home.

Give space with silence.
Let the traditions speak.

All that was needed for life
was well understood
before the Doctrine of Discovery
planted its sword and claimed
that the land
was empty
for God's sake
and God's people.

The deeds outlined
the tools of the colonizer:
*   civilized farming,*
*   fences to prevent wandering,*
*   crosses to save souls.*
Attempts to restrain a people who thrived.

All that was needed for life
was already here.

1. Indigenous peoples have the right to determine and develop priorities and strategies for the development or use of their lands or territories and other resources.

2. States shall consult and cooperate in good faith with the indigenous peoples concerned through their own representative institutions in order to obtain their free and informed consent prior to the approval of any project affecting their lands or territories and other resources, particularly in connection with the development, utilization or exploitation of mineral, water, or other resources.

3. States shall provide effective mechanisms for just and fair redress for any such activities, and appropriate measures shall be taken to mitigate adverse environmental, economic, social, cultural, or spiritual impact.

Be careful young man.
You the one wearing ribbon shirts
and eagle feathers.
Don't get lost in the school of separation.
The universities, the cities,
the worlds of fortune and fame.

My economics professor at Stanford told me
that greed is good.
The chairman of the tribe has decided
he can represent The People.
But is he any better than the colonizer
if he forgot the lessons of the land
while he was away
at business school?

Moving oil
means moving all of creation
out of the way,
the market's opinion the only thing
that matters.

33

1. Indigenous peoples have the right to determine their own identity or membership in accordance with their customs and traditions. This does not impair the right of indigenous individuals to obtain citizenship of the States in which they live.

2. Indigenous peoples have the right to determine the structures and to select the membership of their institutions in accordance with their own procedures.

Rise, People of the Wild Rice.
Rise, People of the Red Willow.
Rise, People of the Middle River.
Rise, People of the Aguaje Palm.
Rise, Lafkenche.
Rise, Pehueche.
Rise. Rise, Mapuche.
Rise, Kahniakehake.

Rise. All of you rise to speak your truth.
We need more people who name themselves
after the land, instead of naming the land
after themselves.

Learn, Washington.
Learn, Georgia.
Learn, Louisville.
Learn, San Luis Obispo.

There is a vast world,
unbeknownst to you (for now).
Climb to the mountain top.
Look out into the valleys.
See just how much you do not
and cannot control.

For too long the solution has been either/or:
  Turn in your status card for the privilege
  of being Canadian.

The alternative absorbs Indigenous identities in Canadiana,
  offering the promise that assimilation is a gift.

Both are solutions
offered by the colonizer
seeking to fulfill our vision
of nationhood.

It is not our decision to enforce.

Indigenous peoples have the right to promote, develop, and maintain their institutional structures and their distinctive customs, spirituality, traditions, procedures, practices, and, in the cases where they exist, juridical systems or customs, in accordance with international human rights standards.

On any given day you
can find Trisha Moquino
working in the classroom, cultivating
little seeds with bright brown eyes, smiles
so wide, open minds, open hands.
They speak their dreams to the daylight
in the Keres language.

She is nourishing their minds,
their bodies, their speech.
Linguistic diversity in the age of extinction.
Like the cottonwood trees,
like the rare desert rivers, prayer births
the sustainability of genes and languages.

Those who seek conquest
have their backs turned to her.
They are lost in business,
busy-ness, busy building
a cemetery for the unborn.
When will they stop
and help her plant the seeds?
When will they see it is time to nourish
what their grandparents worked so hard
to destroy? Even dead soil can be revived
when we work together.

Too often we fear distinction
brings disruption.
Maybe it does.
But that which disrupts also
   opens eyes to diversity,
   births an abundance of possibility,
   enriches our awareness of life.

Indigenous peoples have the right to determine the responsibilities of individuals to their communities.

When the city leaves you purposeless,
and you find yourself at the bottom
of a bottle, and the Spirit
reminds you of your ability and purpose,
responsibility (to a People,
to the waiting earth)
becomes your saviour.

Go out and fight, warrior.
We will always be at your side,
even in the middle of the battlefield.

It is rare for the colonizer to recognize
community. The individual triumph
of God and man
takes the place of honour.
The village that is supposed
to raise the child
locks their doors before bed, while
advertisers ply their trade.

36

1. Indigenous peoples, in particular those divided by international borders, have the right to maintain and develop contacts, relations and cooperation, including activities for spiritual, cultural, political, economic, and social purposes, with their own members as well as other peoples across borders.

2. States, in consultation and cooperation with indigenous peoples, shall take effective measures to facilitate the exercise and ensure the implementation of this right.

The Nakota water protectors
are in Cuetzalan to teach and to learn.
The condors are circling overhead.
We are the same.
We are different.
We are stronger together.

The longest undefended border does not matter
when you need a passport to cross
manufactured divides.
The political ideologies of the colonizer
    draw the line,
    sever the treaty,
    transgress tradition.

37

1. Indigenous peoples have the right to the recognition, observance, and enforcement of treaties, agreements, and other constructive arrangements concluded with States or their successors and to have States honour and respect such treaties, agreements, and other constructive arrangements.

2. Nothing in this Declaration may be interpreted as diminishing or eliminating the rights of indigenous peoples contained in treaties, agreements, and other constructive arrangements.

How do we change the meaning
of the word treaty?
It used to mean "supreme law
of the land."
It used to mean "solemn agreement
and promise."
Now it means "old piece of paper
that people ignore."

The business man and the government,
they are one and the same,
carrying a doctrine
of false progress.
They think they are winning
when they get away
with ignoring the treaties.
But they are losing
in the most profound way
they can lose.

Integrity, honour, is worth more
than money in the final analysis.
We sit back and they say we are losing.
But we have lost nothing.
We retain our honesty.
We have lost nothing. Nothing
at all.

Covenant.
Archaic agreements to some.
Signs of defeat for others.

The land of the treaties
is not our promised land.
It never was.

38

States, in consultation and cooperation with indigenous peoples, shall take the appropriate measures, including legislative measures, to achieve the ends of this Declaration.

The UNDRIP puts our principles
into the format of the numbed world.
It begins to speak of the Sacred.
To achieve its goal, the numbed world
must come into the format of the sweat lodge.

For some things cannot be explained
in words or written into books.
They must be understood through the body.

I will try to tell you
about the person I love.
The way they speak.
The way they hold me.
The way they love me too.
But you will never understand love
until you fall in love for yourself.
Only then will you understand
its power. Its beauty. Its sanctity.

These words are signs on the road
telling you where to go. They are not
the destination.

Much of the work is our responsibility
but it is not ours to control.
These words do not chart a path
to reconciliation.
They are an invitation to relationship.
  A gift.
  A summons.

39

Indigenous peoples have the right to have access to financial and technical assistance from States and, through international cooperation, for the enjoyment of the rights contained in this Declaration.

We tell you to help us rebuild
our communities after you dropped
bombs on our roof tops.
We did not tell you that your help
was not for us.
We did not need you to rebuild
the walls of our homes.
You needed you to rebuild
your beauty and honour.
Only when we build together
will we heal together.

These walls are not the destination.
They are the road to sisterhood.
The road to brotherhood.

When awareness shifts,
the word looms in front of me:
Colonizer.
My blindness is my shame.
My sorrow not enough.
There is a cost to right relationship.

Yet, action is not a burden.
It does not demand all things.
It honours vulnerability.
It trusts the Spirit
    and brings beauty as it heals.

40

ARTICLE 40

Indigenous peoples have the right to access to and prompt decision through just and fair procedures for the resolution of conflicts and disputes with States or other parties, as well as to effective remedies for all infringements of their individual and collective rights. Such a decision shall give due consideration to the customs, traditions, rules, and legal systems of the indigenous peoples concerned and international human rights.

Only when we love
in the face of hatred
can we loosen the screws
of the machine of oppression.
For who stands unphased
in the face of grace?
Only the expertly numb.

The rest of the world, the majority,
trembles in the best of ways.
They are shaken. They are
inspired. They are transformed.
They are forgiven.
This is the truest,
most lasting,
justice.

Two years to complete
an inquiry for murdered and missing women
after some families went years without
a phone call.

What hope can be offered
when the justice system has already spoken:
"She was known to run away.
She was engaged in a high-risk lifestyle.
70 percent of Indigenous women are
    killed by Indigenous men."

Violence is considered
a tragic side effect
of being an Indigenous woman.

Consultation is an empty promise
when actions grind to a halt.

41

The organs and specialized agencies of the United Nations system and other intergovernmental organizations shall contribute to the full realization of the provisions of this Declaration through the mobilization, *inter alia*, of financial cooperation and technical assistance. Ways and means of ensuring participation of indigenous peoples on issues affecting them shall be established.

We said we wanted "a seat
at the table."
What we meant is
we want you to come and sit
by the river.

The dichotomy of Indigenous
and non-Indigenous
is false. And only when
we all realize our own indigenousity
can we live as the equals we are.

The UN is on board.
That means something I suppose.
But the debates and decisions
around official tables
(under the umbrella of world peace)
rarely influence our conversations at dinner.
The long journey from a
non-binding declaration
to life
will only be made
if those in my own house
take steps to fulfill the call.

42

ARTICLE 42

The United Nations, its bodies, including the Permanent Forum on Indigenous Issues, and specialized agencies, including at the country level, and States shall promote respect for and full application of the provisions of this Declaration and follow up the effectiveness of this Declaration.

We said we wanted "influence."
What we mean is don't look: See.
What we mean is don't listen: Hear.
What we mean is don't touch: Feel.
What we mean is don't eat: Taste.
What we mean is don't think: Be.

What we mean is, come down
from your office building.
Stop scraping the sky like a hungry
sucker fish. Unplug yourself
from your worries.
There is a radiant song
from every leaf, every stone,
and it even sings beneath the thin veil
of pavement that somehow separates
you from the blaring symphony of creation.
Look up from your phone and see.

Next steps:
be self-aware,
disrupt,
offer care,
move

with love,
both as foundation
and greatest height.

43

The rights recognized herein constitute the minimum standards for the survival, dignity, and well-being of the indigenous peoples of the world.

Please do not call this land America.
If you listen you will hear
her true name as the nighthawks
dive at twilight.
As the wolves howl at moonlight.
As the waterfalls rage, cascading.
As the avalanches fracture, breaking.

She will tell you her true name
with earthquakes that split states and break
fences to remind you she does not belong to you.

We cannot write your rights on a paper
and you cannot write ours either.
They are written into the bark of trees.
They are written
in the silence between you and me.
Still we try like fumbling humans
and, no matter its shortcomings,
there is the honour we seek.
The honour we need to breathe.

It is disquieting:
the basic requirements for dignity,
the minimum standards for respect,
need to be written down.

What does a written word make true?
Words become flesh when they are lived.

44

ARTICLE 44

All the rights and freedoms recognized herein are equally guaranteed to male and female indigenous individuals.

The Cree have said all
there is to say:
"A nation is not defeated until the hearts
of the women are on the ground."

Humanity fully embraced as equals:
    This is still a dream
    but it should be embodied,
    giving life and breath to truth.
Strangers no more.

Nothing in this Declaration may be construed as diminishing or extinguishing the rights indigenous peoples have now or may acquire in the future.

We patiently await the day
when our collective love for morality
robs the stalk and root
from the thorns of inequity.

The way forward is a gift
offered time and again.
Invitations to relationship have been met
with the foundations of prejudice:
  disinterest,
  denial,
  defensiveness,
  distrust.
We can seek a good mind together.
It is time.

ARTICLE 46

1. Nothing in this Declaration may be interpreted as implying for any State, people, group, or person any right to engage in any activity or to perform any act contrary to the Charter of the United Nations or construed as authorizing or encouraging any action which would dismember or impair, totally or in part, the territorial integrity or political unity of sovereign and independent States.

2. In the exercise of the rights enunciated in the present Declaration, human rights and fundamental freedoms of all shall be respected. The exercise of the rights set forth in this Declaration shall be subject only to such limitations as are determined by law and in accordance with international human rights obligations. Any such limitations shall be non-discriminatory and strictly necessary solely for the purpose of securing due recognition and respect for the rights and freedoms of others and for meeting the just and most compelling requirements of a democratic society.

3. The provisions set forth in this Declaration shall be interpreted in accordance with the principles of justice, democracy, respect for human rights, equality, non-discrimination, good governance, and good faith.

Time will tell the course
of our collective.
We are one in the end.

Some are parrots.
Some are falcons.
Some are cranes.
And some are pigeons.

But at sunset, we are all birds
needing a place to roost, a nest
to shield us from the winter wind.
See me in you. See you in me.

We will learn this hard lesson
together.
Some will starve. Some will overeat.
Some will freeze. Some will overheat.
Recycled souls evaporate
then drop against the parched
canvas of the earth, smelling
like the sweet aspiration of
a trillion lives lived.

Love sustains us. Love recreates us.
Love remains after all the blood,
and all the pain.

Love remains.
Love remains.

When superiority is silenced,
beauty is seen.
    Movement, risk,
    relationship, love.

In communion:
    movement.

In vulnerability:
    risk.

In hearing:
    relationship.

In sharing:
    love.

Let us be who
we were created to be.

No Reconciliation without Justice

As Canada attempts to move towards reconciliation, it needs to come to grips both with its violent colonial history and its ongoing human rights violations against Indigenous peoples. Rooted in racist legislation and paternalistic policies, such as the Indian Act, the federal government has wilfully, indifferently, and systemically transgressed basic and fundamental Indigenous human rights.

We see not-so-distant examples of these violations in the Indian residential school system (which was run throughout "the Dominion" primarily between the 1870s and the 1970s) and the 60's Scoop (the mass adoption of "Indian and Métis" children). Thousands of children were taken away from their families, communities, and cultures, leaving them in foreign environments, often void of affection and riddled with abuse—physical, sexual, emotional, and spiritual.

We witness contemporary instances of such human rights transgressions in inequitable funding for Indigenous peoples residing on reserve. Basic needs, like housing, clean water, education, and healthcare are not adequately provided—not in the ways they are for Settler Canadians. The result is significantly higher rates of poverty that leave many Indigenous peoples homeless on our ancestral lands. And Indigenous children are the ones that suffer the most.

Canada is one of the wealthiest and most privileged countries in the world. Yet it is currently in the midst of a child welfare crisis. There are now more Indigenous children in care than at the height of the residential school era. In Manitoba, where I reside, more than 90 percent of the children in Child and Family Services are Indigenous, even though we represent only 17 percent of the province's population. That amounts to almost 10,000 children in care. How is this possible? The answer is obvious for those whose hearts have been pushed to the ground. It's a result of blatant human rights violations against Indigenous families and communities by successive Settler governments. Canadian genocide is not a thing of the past. It continues today.

According to Article 2 of the *United Nations Convention on the Prevention and Punishment of the Crime of Genocide* (1948), acts of genocide include:

a. Killing members of the group
b. Causing serious bodily or mental harm to members of the group
c. Deliberately inflicting on the group conditions of life calculated to bring about its physical destruction in whole or in part
d. Imposing measures intended to prevent births within the group
e. Forcibly transferring children of the group to another group.

It is a hard and awful truth for many Canadians, but it must be faced. Canada's dirty little secret is that it continues to commit genocidal acts against Indigenous peoples — institutionalized poverty, the relentless theft and exploitation of traditional lands, the repeated fracture of families and cultures. These acts must be acknowledged and then addressed, with substance, before we can truly achieve reconciliation in these home and native lands that not all of us call "Canada." There is no reconciliation in the absence of justice. Until Canada takes immediate action to support the fundamental human rights of Indigenous peoples, the oft-proclaimed desire to right the wrongs of the past will stand as rhetoric at best.

In June 2015, the Truth and Reconciliation Commission (TRC) on Indian Residential Schools — a seven-year effort led by Indigenous survivors to educate the public about Canada's colonial story and its impact on Indigenous-Settler relationships — put forth its *94 Calls to Action*. The *Calls* provide a path forward, articulating what various societal bodies (churches, corporations, governments, media, and so on) need to do in order to repair what has been broken and return what was lost. At the centre of the *Calls* we find the *United Nations Declaration on the Rights of Indigenous Peoples* and the clear summons for its full adoption and implementation. The *Declaration* is lifted up as the framework for reconciliation, the way in which the spirit and intent of the sacred Treaty tradition — an integral but largely forgotten history — can actually be realized. Lifted up in no less than 16 of the *Calls to Action*, the TRC contends that the principles and inherent rights recognized in the *Declaration* must be honoured by Canada before we can move toward a renewed nation-to-nation relationship, let alone work for the survival of many of our nations.

The poetry in this publication speaks to the urgency of our present situation and the importance of the *Declaration*. Lyla June Johnston and Joy De Vito summon us to collective, neighbourly, land-connected action in order to nurture relations of respect, mutuality, and friendship. They warn us not to put our hope in states or to wait on governments to take the lead. My heart beats alongside them. Though Indigenous peoples are often admonished by Settler society to be patient, to give them time, and more time, in the expectation that things might move, eventually, in a good way...the time has certainly come. We cannot wait any longer.

There is a pressing need to shift Canada's history of Indigenous human rights violations—violations that cripple our nations and the lands and waters we all depend on. Change is possible. Indigenous peoples are becoming increasingly organized in their fight against neo-colonialism. Many Settlers are doing their decolonizing homework and their voices are growing stronger in support of Indigenous peoples human rights. Together, the elusive talk of reconciliation is slowly becoming more tangible. My hope is that the politically privileged and powerful will do the right thing and join this growing grassroots movement; that they will start to walk the talk of reconciliation, beginning with an embrace of the *Declaration*'s minimum standards.

Minimum standards. Nothing fancy. We're asking only for what is fair and just and human.

I recently crafted a poem in honour of someone very dear to me who never experienced such minimum standards. I have a lot of poems like this. It shouldn't be like this. It doesn't need to be. We can do otherwise.

The Flower

He said he never received flowers
A blossomed heart
An orchard to be cherished

He said he never received flowers
A spirit they tried to break
In residential school

Behinds walls
That grew weeds of genocide
There were no flowers

They had no flowers
For an artist's spirit
Whose creativity was born out of kindness

He said he never received flowers
A spirit so worthy to be embraced
By kindness and love

So here is your flower
Let the smells fill your room
With the beauty of your sacred heart

Leah Gazan
Educator and grassroots mobilizer
Wood Mountain Lakota Nation, Treaty 4 Territory

To order additional copies of *Lifting Hearts Off the Ground*
or other resources on Indigenous rights and decolonization,
visit: commonword.ca